Earth ! Earth ! Earth !

A collection of nature poetry.

James Burns

Earth ! Earth ! Earth !

DEDICATION

Clodoaldo Barrera

Jessica Burnett

Donna Cusano

Julie Gomez

Anne Lynch

Kate Norris

Carl Prine

Deanna Prine

Robert Ronimus

Janet Sutter

Joe Sutter

Susan Tweit

1.

Our snow laden tree

The one the smaller birds loved

The tree that shaded the rabbits

Snapped this morning

By nature's unforgiving hand.

2.

If I prune my beliefs

And change who I am

Bend and twist my soul

As if I were the maker's bonsai tree

If I give way to your will

What then becomes of me ?

3.

Our love is an old veneer

Cracked, faded, and torn

Scratched away from our life

By sharp words and harsh reality.

4.

Many winters ago

We said our goodbyes

I left with my life

Leaving only impressions in the snow.

5.

I am reborn with your love

It has sent me

To kite high

portions of the sky.

6.

How painted is our love ?

We applied a coat last winter

When it was cold

Now it cracks and falls away.

7.

Wind rider

You are swift in your desire

Let us chase dreams together

High, between the clouds.

8.

I don't want to be your shooting star

Always at a distance, and never at your side

I'd rather be the soil beneath your feet

Always fertile, ready, complete.

9.

Coronado beach

As a youth I walked her skin

I sat with her to understand

The softness that we call sand.

10.

Writing away the pain

Like rain against a dirty door

The mud knows not to explain.

11.

Clumps of matter, brown and gray

Dandelions intermingle, proud at play

Freshly laid from life they sprung

On pasture land – they are but dung.

12.

Assume that I love you

Presume that I care

Resume with your slumber

I'll never be there.

13.

Human life is a lace on the shoe of death

Do not hesitate to embrace love

For soon our life is tied

And we are walked away.

14.

The sound of rain turning to hail

Against my window

Hard and harsh.

The sound of my past actions

Hitting my heart

Hard and harsh.

15.

Polar bears and grizzly bears

Mate to form grolars and pizzlies

How it's done and if it's fun

Could make my mind go dizzily.

16.

"What happens to my fist

When I open my hand?"

What happens to my anger

When I understand ?

What happens to my soul

When I open my mind ?

What happens to the world

When I decide to be kind ?

17.

We paint our own picture of reality

From the palette and brushes

We were given as children

Our canvass won't last forever

Neither will friendship

Neither will love.

18.

The transcendental mind

Knows God through nature

And sees what most won't see

His masterwork, our planet Earth.

19.

What became of my dreams ?

They were so blue sky big

So packed

Tightly overflowing

So sure, so exciting

What became of them ?

20.

A half-life ago

I was radiant with desire.

I believed that numbers

And science held my future.

Alchemy did not change me

Nor the world.

Water overcame fire.

Wind will soon yield to earth.

21.

Welcome home

To a stained glass window

You fit in the far left corner.

22.

'Twas the night of the asteroid

And earth was asleep

The governors ignored it

That rock played for keeps.

Made in the USA
Las Vegas, NV
04 September 2023

77058137R00015